Tell Me What for Use These

Language and cognitive development

for

4 - 5 years

Copyright © 2022 by A Devi Thangamaniam.

All right reserved. No part of this publication may be reproduced, distributed, or transmitted in any form or by any means, including photocopying, recording, or other electronic or mechanical methods, without the prior written permission of the author, except in the case of brief quotations embodied in critical reviews and certain other non-commercial uses permitted by copyright law.

Information: MiLu Children's Educational Source.
www.my-willing.com
ISBN: 979 8 88525 428 1

Tell Me What for

Use These

Who knows?

Fill in the words and tell me verbally.

School starts in the morning.

Lucas needs to ride.
He needs a **bike.**
Bike for **riding.**

The car is in the parking spot.

Varan needs to drive.
He needs . . .
Car for . . .

The painting brushes are on the table.

Amu needs to paint.
She needs . . .
Painting brushes for . . .

Mia is in the backyard.

Mia needs to play.
She needs . . .
Ball for . . .

The puppy is barking.

The puppy needs to eat.
The puppy needs . . .
Food for . . .

The apple is tasty.

I need to eat.
I need . . .
Apple for . . .

The papers are on the creative table.

> Lilly needs to cut.
> She needs . . .
> Scissors for . . .

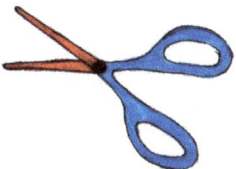

This is an interesting story.

> Tommy needs to read.
> She needs . . .
> Books for . . .

Lia has some pencils.

> Lia needs to write.
> She needs . . .
> Pencils for . . .

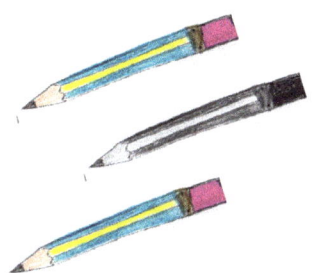

Kindergartens are going to play musical chairs.

Kindergartens need to sit.
They need . . .
Chairs for . . .

The puzzles are on the carpet.

I need to fix.
I need . . .
Puzzles for . . .

Grandpa is tired.

Grandpa needs to sleep.
He needs . . .
Bed for . . .

It's raining outside.

> I need to hold.
> I need . . .
> Umbrella for . . .

There are some blocks on the carpet.

> Kaya needs to construct.
> She needs . . .
> Blocks for . . .

Today is Jonny's birthday.

> Thanvir needs to decorate.
> He needs . . .
> Balloons for . . .

Monkeys are under the banana tree.

The monkeys need to eat.
They need . . .
Bananas for . . .

Photos are in the photo albums.

Pre-schoolers need to look.
They need . . .
Photo albums for . . .

There is a long table.

I need to measure.
I need . . .
Ruler for . . .

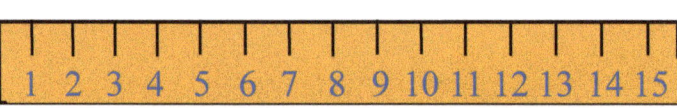

Skipping rope is hanging on the wall.

    My sister needs to skip.
    She needs . . .
    Skipping rope for . . .

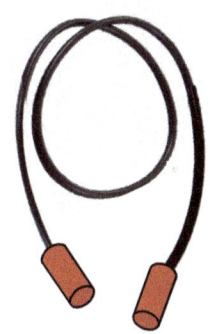

There is a mirror in the room.

    Veema needs to look.
    He needs . . .
    Mirror for . . .

It's the hot sun on the outside.

    Nina needs to wear.
    She needs . . .
    Hat for . . .

There are some errors in the letter.

My brother needs to erase.

He needs . . .

Eraser for . . .

The sofa is in the living room.

Sana needs to sit.

She needs . . .

Sofa for . . .

Muru works on the computer.

Muru needs to type.

He needs . . .

Keyboard for . . .

The floor is wet.

> My brother needs to mop.
> He needs . . .
> Mopper for . . .

My teacher is making bubble soap.

> I need to blow.
> I need . . .
> Bubble stick for . . .

The spring season is starting.

> Famers need to crop plants.
> They need . . .
> Seeds for . . .

My hands are dirty.

My hands need to clean.
I need . . .
Hand soap for . . .

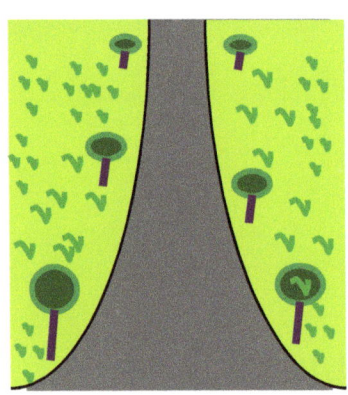

My mom goes to the library.

My mom needs to walk.
She needs . . .
Sidewalk for . . .

Vaani wants to know the date.

Vaani needs to look.
She needs . . .
Calendar for . . .

January 2021

M	T	W	T	F	S	S
				1	2	3
4	5	6	7	8	9	10
11	12	13	14	15	16	17
18	19	20	21	22	23	24
25	26	27	28	29	30	31

It's cold outside.

Toddlers need to wear.
They need . . .
Mittens for . . .

The time is ten o clock.

The teacher needs to look.
She needs . . .
Clock for . . .

The baby is crying.

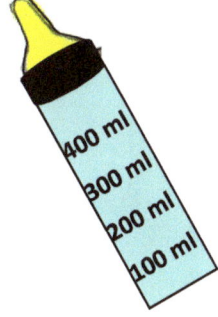

The baby needs to drink.
She needs . . .
Milk for . . .

The traffic signal light is on the road.

>People need to go.
>They need to wait for the . . .
>Green light for . . .

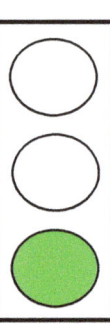

The balancing beam is in the playground.

Kindergartens need to balance.
They need . . .
Balancing beam for . . .

There is a swing in the park.

>I need to swing.
>I need . . .
>Swing for . . .

The floor is dirty.

> Lei needs to sweep.
> He needs . . .
> Broom for . . .

My brother likes to wear sweaters.

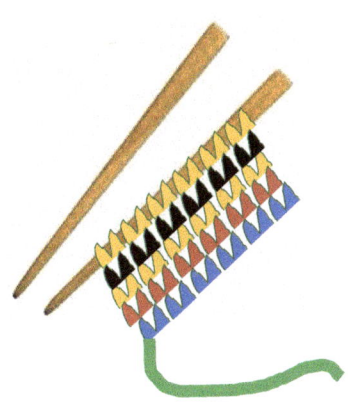

> My grandma needs to knit.
> She needs . . .
> Knitting needles for . . .

Babies like to listen.

> I need to shake.
> I need . . .
> Shakers for . . .

The flour is in the bowl.

Maali needs to measure.

She needs . . .

Measuring cup for . . .

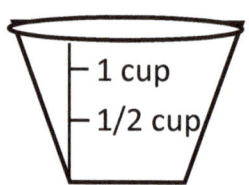

My uncle has toothpaste.

He needs to brush.

He needs . . .

Toothbrush for . . .

My shirt is on the chair.

I need to hang.

I need . . .

Hanger for . . .

We are in the park.

We need to look.
We need . . .
Flowers for . . .

Juice is in the glass.

My brother needs to drink.
He needs . . .
Juice for . . .

It's wonderful music.

Brother needs to play.
He needs . . .
Guitar for . . .

17

Yeah!

You got it.

Wonderful attempt.

www.ingramcontent.com/pod-product-compliance
Lightning Source LLC
LaVergne TN
LVHW072133060526
838201LV00072B/5026